IMAGES
of America

McGuire
Air Force Base

Famous children's television host Rex Trainer and his horse Gold Rush entertain McGuire Air Force Base children in February 1955. Trainer was an icon in the Northeast until the late 1960s.

IMAGES
of America

McGuire
Air Force Base

G.W. Boyd

ARCADIA

First printed in 2003.

Published by Arcadia Publishing,
an imprint of Tempus Publishing Inc.
2A Cumberland Street
Charleston, SC 29401

Printed in Great Britain.

Library of Congress Catalog Card Number: 2002116971

For all general information, contact Arcadia Publishing:
Telephone 843-853-2070
Fax 843-853-0044
E-mail sales@arcadiapublishing.com

For customer service and orders:
Toll-free 1-888-313-2665

Visit us on the Internet at www.arcadiapublishing.com.

American Bandstand host Dick Clark, singer Cathy Linden, and musical group Jimmy J. and the Js entertained throngs of fans at McGuire in May 1959 for Armed Forces Day. (McGuire Air Force Base History Office.)

CONTENTS

ACKNOWLEDGMENTS

This book is possible only through the work of numerous military photographers, historians, and archivists through the years around the world. I especially want to thank Dr. Dan Zimmerman of the Fort Dix Museum; Carolee Nesbitt of the Fort Dix Public Affairs Office; Betsy Conzo, who assisted me from the McGuire Air Force Base History Office; and Cathi Cooper and Capt. John Dorrian of the McGuire Air Force Base Public Affairs Office, who steered this project to me. One man, however, especially stands out: Don Spering of AIR Hobbies in Mount Holly, New Jersey, who has been one of the great supporters of McGuire Air Force Base through the years. He has been taking photographs of the base and its aircraft for over 50 years and generously allowed me to use some of his work. Much of his work has been incorporated into the permanent archives of the U.S. Air Force.

This book is dedicated to the men and women who helped make McGuire great, and I have donated all my benefits from this work to the base library and airmen's projects. Obviously, I owe a huge debt of gratitude to my family, especially to my wife, Leatha, who tolerated my nights and weekends at the computer trying to pull this work together. I also extend my gratitude to Col. Randall Lanning, a great supporter of U.S. Air Force history, who encouraged me to take on this project.

—G.W. Boyd
January 2003

INTRODUCTION

TEAM MCGUIRE

The genesis of McGuire Air Force Base is rooted in the establishment of Fort Dix during World War I. Then known as Camp Dix, it quickly became one of the most important mobilization training bases in the United States in 1917. After the war, the huge reservation continued in use as a large training ground. The first probable aircraft landing on what later comprised McGuire occurred during a mock invasion of New Jersey during maneuvers in 1925. Thereafter, an unimproved airstrip cut into the pastureland, adorned with merely a windsock and located near what became the Aero Club, augmented the infantry training under way at Fort Dix.

In 1937, in the midst of the Great Depression, the Civilian Conservation Corps built encampments on the land and later built improved concrete airstrips. The new airfield for Fort Dix was named after Guy K. Rudd, a Newark aviator who lost his life in an air crash in 1931. Rudd Field became part of the ambitious expansion plans of the U.S. Army Air Corps, and the War Department redesignated it as Fort Dix Army Air Base in 1939. It supported the training of recently activated National Guard observation units. By 1942, Fort Dix Army Airfield and nearly 15,000 acres of Fort Dix property passed to the new U.S. Army Air Forces. Aircraft such as the O-47, O-52, B-24, and B-25 flew from Fort Dix Army Airfield on important antisubmarine patrols, guarding the approaches to New York City, the port at Bayonne, the Philadelphia Naval Yards, and Atlantic City. As World War II wound down, the base became the eastern terminal for returning wounded from Europe and thousands of separating troops. By October 1946, all U.S. Army Air Forces operations ended on Fort Dix Army Airfield. The dormant status of the base was temporary; the cold war and the base's strategic location between huge metropolitan areas ensured its further use.

The U.S. Air Force reopened the base in September 1948, and it was dedicated as McGuire Air Force Base in honor of the late Maj. Thomas B. McGuire Jr., who was a Medal of Honor recipient, the second leading ace in American history, and a New Jersey native born in Ridgewood. Initially, the 91st Reconnaissance Wing of Strategic Air Command (SAC) was stationed here with RB-29 and RB-50 reconnaissance aircraft. Later, Air Defense Command and the 52nd Fighter Interceptor Wing took over with F-82, F-94, and F-86 jet fighters, joined by the New Jersey Air National Guard in 1951.

In 1954, a seismic shift in missions occurred at McGuire—an orientation that has lasted almost 50 years. The 1611th Air Transport Wing arrived with C-54 Skymaster and C-118 Liftmaster transports, under command of the Military Air Transport Service (MATS). In addition, Navy Air Transport squadrons augmented the MATS contingent with the R6D, their version of the C-118. Together, they provided passenger and cargo service to Europe and were key in the evacuation of refugees after the Hungarian revolution failed in 1956. In 1962, the U.S. Air Force's only C-135 jet transports were assigned. In 1964, the C-130E entered service with U.S. Air Force and U.S. Navy transport squadrons, replacing the C-118. With the departure of the navy from MATS in 1966, MATS became the Military Airlift Command (MAC), and the 438th Military Airlift Wing replaced the 1611th Air Transport Wing. C-141s began arriving in 1967, replacing the C-135s and C-130s by 1968. During the Vietnam War, McGuire aircrews transported troops and supplies to South Vietnam and, in 1973, airlifted prisoners of war from North Vietnam.

McGuire personnel participated in the Beirut Marine barracks bombing airlift, the Grenada rescue effort, and the invasion of Panama in the 1980s. They were also a part of the subsequent support of operations in Haiti. Beginning in August 1990, McGuire units supported Operation Desert Shield, the defense of Saudi Arabia. Aircrews and deployed support members began supporting Operation Desert Storm in January 1991. Combat ceased in February, followed by the massive withdrawal of troops and equipment for Operation Desert Calm beginning in March. In May 1991, McGuire aircrews began delivering food and supplies to Turkey under Operation Provide Comfort, supplying Iraqi Kurd refugees in southern Turkey and northern Iraq.

On June 1, 1992, McGuire became a major part of the newly activated Air Mobility Command, made up of former MAC airlift and SAC tanker units. From 1992 to August 31, 1994, McGuire developed, trained, and operated the C-141B Special Operations Low-Level II program, supporting a wide variety of interservice users, a mission that recently returned to McGuire with the conversion to the C-17 at Charleston Air Force Base, South Carolina.

From December 1992 to May 1993, McGuire supported Operation Restore Hope as personnel were deployed to Cairo, Egypt, and Mogadishu in December to set up operations and control the flow of aircraft in the peacekeeping-humanitarian effort for famine-stricken Somalia. McGuire aircrew and ground personnel played a critical role in airlifting the bulk of the 28,000 military troops and equipment to Somalia, as well as in resupply operations, troop movements, and in May 1993, the redeployment of troops.

In July 1993, the base was selected by Air Mobility Command officials to become the East Coast air mobility wing. As a result, the first of 24 McDonnell Douglas KC-10 Extender tanker-cargo aircraft and three C-12 Huron aircraft arrived in September 1994.

In December 1993, Air Mobility Command officials selected nearby Fort Dix Army Reserve Base as the new location for the Air Mobility Warfare Center, which opened in June 1994—a mission supported by Team McGuire.

In October 1995, personnel and aircraft from McGuire were deployed to Germany and the Balkan region in support of Operation Joint Endeavor, the implementation of a peace settlement in war-torn Boznia-Herzegovina. The wing played a major role in the deployment of more than 20,000 U.S. troops into the region and continues support of this ongoing operation.

The men and women of McGuire continue to be in the forefront of high-visibility operations with regular deployments of airlift and aerial refueling aircraft and support elements for combat operations, including Allied Force (over Kosovo) and Operations Northern and Southern Watch (enforcing no-fly zones over Iraq). Just as visible are humanitarian relief and disaster-response operations, including airlift missions to Central America and the Caribbean after Hurricanes Georges and Mitch in 1998 and recent flooding in Mozambique. McGuire supported Operation Enduring Freedom from the opening minutes of the tragic events of September 11, 2001. Team McGuire personnel can be found at virtually any U.S. Air Force contingency base worldwide.

THE THOMAS B. MCGUIRE JR. STORY

Maj. Thomas B. McGuire Jr., in whose memory McGuire was dedicated in 1948, was born in Ridgewood on August 1, 1920. His father, Thomas B. McGuire Sr., owned a Packard automobile dealership in Patterson, and the family was fairly affluent during the Great Depression. After his parents separated, he moved with his mother in the 1930s to Sebring, Florida, where he spent his teenage years. An accomplished clarinet player and driver, McGuire was accepted as an engineering student at the Georgia Institute of Technology (Georgia Tech University). Nonetheless, the promising student forsook personal gain when he left college in his third year to join the U.S. Army Air Forces in 1941 as an aviation cadet. Very slight of build (less than 140 pounds and 5 feet 8 inches tall), he made up in determination what he lacked in size.

A quick study and a natural pilot, McGuire flew pursuit-type aircraft in World War II. His first operational assignment was flying patrols over the Aleutian Islands and Alaska in the P-39 Airacobra with the 54th Pursuit Group from June to December 1942. Returning to the U.S. "Zone of the Interior," McGuire transitioned to the P-38 Lightning. He also married Marilynn Giesler, a San Antonio native he had fallen in love with during his time in pilot training. In March 1943, he was sent to the south Pacific as a P-38H Lightning pilot with the 49th Fighter Group, 5th Air Force. On countless patrols, he saw no air-to-air combat while a member of the 49ers—the unit was dominated by P-40s, and McGuire and his companions generally flew high cover missions for the Warhawks.

Five months later, he was sent to the 431st Fighter Squadron (Satan's Angels) of Gen. George Kenney's all-P-38 475th Fighter Group—the first such group to form in the 5th Air Force and activate overseas. McGuire's many hundreds of hours of routine flying proved to be an invaluable apprenticeship when he did enter combat. On August 18, 1943, McGuire was part of a group flying top cover for bombers striking at Wewak, New Guinea. Nearing their target, the fighters were attacked by Japanese aircraft. During the battle, McGuire shot down two Ki-43 II Oscars and one Ki-61 Tony. On the following day, near the same location, he downed two more Oscars. This established him as an air ace after engaging the enemy only twice. His score thereafter rose very quickly, and some say he was the most gifted combat pilot in U.S. Air Force history. Such is not mere hyperbole; many victories came against highly maneuverable fighters in the less-than-agile P-38 flown to its very maximum capability. It was not unusual for McGuire's wingmen to black out or lose their leader during his combat maneuvering. By the end of 1944, McGuire had scored 38 aerial victories, still the second highest of all time. He was poised to become the U.S. Air Force's leading ace until fate intervened.

On January 7, 1945, McGuire was leading a group of four P-38s over the Japanese-held Fabrica airstrip on Negros Islands, the Philippines. His formation scattered by rough weather conditions, McGuire and his wingman dove on a Ki-43 Oscar aircraft at low level. Unfortunately, the Oscar was piloted by a Japanese pilot with thousands of hours of experience (quite unusual for that point in the war). McGuire dove on the plane with drop tanks still in place; in the wild turning melee that followed, another Japanese aircraft, a superb Ki-84 Frank, entered the dogfight unobserved. McGuire's P-38 apparently entered a low-speed unrecoverable stall at low level while attempting to clear the tail of his wingman, Lt. Edwin Weaver. His plane crashed, inverted, a few miles from the Fabrica airstrip near a village. Ironically, McGuire met his death not in his famous 131 *Pudgy V* (a restored P-38 in this livery is on display at McGuire), but rather in Capt. Fred Champlin's 112 *Eileen Anne*. McGuire had felt *Pudgy* V had about run out of luck.

McGuire was awarded the Medal of Honor posthumously for his final mission and for missions on December 25 and 26, in which he shot down seven Japanese fighters. He is the highest-ranking American ace ever to have been lost in combat. McGuire's other decorations include the Distinguished Service Cross, 3 silver stars, 6 Distinguished Flying Crosses, 15 Air Medals, and 3 Purple Hearts—all before he was 25. He was that rarest of individuals who achieved many extraordinary goals through sheer will and hard work—a warrior's warrior who graces our midst infrequently.

Movie legend Cleo Moore is crowned queen of the McGuire Mardi Gras on February 5, 1955. Although she died in the 1980s, she still has a cult following for her 18 movies. She was at McGuire to promote Universal's *Hold Back Tomorrow*.

One
ORIGINS

The first flight in North America took off in nearby Philadelphia and landed in Woodbury, New Jersey, in 1793, as commemorated in this proclamation. (McGuire Air Force Base History Office.)

Camp Dix is shown around the time when construction commenced in mid-1917. This picture and the photograph on the following page were taken with a panoramic camera of the period. (Fort Dix Museum Archives.)

Cornfields and farmland dominated the area surrounding Camp Dix. It was as pastoral a setting as could be imagined and was a far cry from many casual observers' opinions of New Jersey as a continuous industrial park. The setting remains quite rural even in the 21st century. (Fort Dix Museum Archives.)

This is believed to be the earliest photograph of air operations at the Camp Dix aerodrome, although the first flights took place in at least 1926 and probably during World War I. The picture was taken in the very early spring of 1930, facing Wrightstown (visible in the background). It shows the 5th Observation Squadron and its O-1 and O-11 aircraft. Camp Dix had reverted to reserve status by this time. (Fort Dix Museum Archives.)

The state established the flying contingent of its National Guard in September 1928, supporting the 44th Army Division. The 119th Observation Squadron became the first permanent air unit in the state, flying O-2H observation aircraft. This view shows the visiting 5th Observation Squadron from Mitchel Field, New York. (Fort Dix Public Affairs.)

A Douglas O-2H is shown on August 21, 1930. It was really on the cusp of the next generation of aircraft but looked like an uprated DeHaviland DH-4. (McGuire Air Force Base History Office.)

Once the improvements of the Civilian Conservation Corps had been completed in 1937 (namely, the addition of the concrete runway), the U.S. Army dedicated the Fort Dix airstrip to 2d Lt. Guy K. Rudd—Rudd Field. Lieutenant Rudd lost his life on December 11, 1932, when his aircraft struck a tree and crashed at Bernardsville after he waited too long to pull out of a low-altitude dive. He had completed flying training in World War I and had flown O-17s and an O-38 like this one in the National Guard. It was in the O-38 that he lost his life. His rear observer, Cpl. Robert W. Junemann, also lost his life but was given no such memorial. (McGuire Air Force Base History Office.)

The interwar period for flying at Camp Dix involved transient air units. The land that later became McGuire Air Force Base housed the Civilian Conservation Corps during the peak of the Great Depression. Although the first aircraft to land and use the airstrip at Fort Dix on a regular basis were assigned to the 119th Observation Squadron (New Jersey Air National Guard at Newark Airport after 1931), the first aircraft to be permanently assigned to Fort Dix Army Air Forces Base, Rudd Field, were North American O-47s, pictured here. (McGuire Air Force Base History Office.)

The first aerial components assigned to McGuire were the 119th and 126th Observation Squadrons (on June 9, 1941), flying the North American O-47 and Stinson O-49 (later redesignated L-1). They were soon joined by the 104th Observation Squadron, flying O-46s such as this one in December 1941, weeks after Pearl Harbor. (McGuire Air Force Base History Office.)

The Curtiss O-52 was another of the observation aircraft stationed in southern New Jersey during the base's early days. By and large, many flying fields established near U.S. Army bases had so-called cooperation aircraft as their mission complement—better to assist the nearby ground forces. (McGuire Air Force Base History Office.)

Two
WORLD WAR II AND FORMAL ESTABLISHMENT

This photograph from the 1943 Fort Dix Army Air Base yearbook shows a B-25C of the 11th Antisubmarine Squadron and an honor detail. The U.S. Navy took over the mission, and the formation could well be the inactivation of the squadron. Note that the Bendix lower turret remains in place on this home-defense aircraft (a feature often removed overseas to save weight). (Fort Dix Museum Archives.)

In 1942, the U.S. Army ground forces relinquished control of the base to the U.S. Army Air Forces under jurisdiction of the 1st Air Force. The base was to be used as a key antisubmarine facility during the height of the Battle of the Atlantic being fought off the coast of the state. The B-24s arrived in mid-1943, wearing the red-surround national insignia of the period. The B-24s followed B-25s and B-34s as the last of the U.S. Army Air Forces antisubmarine aircraft; the U.S. Navy took over the duty after September 1943. (McGuire Air Force Base History Office.)

The 3rd and 11th Antisubmarine Squadrons had detachments flying B-24Ds on Fort Dix Army Air Base in 1943—even the 8th Air Force and several B-17 units staged through the base in 1942 and 1943. (McGuire Air Force Base History Office.)

CONFIDENTIAL

(01-870H-11ARON)(6-14-43-1100)(6"-3000)AIR BASE FT. DIX N.J.

This aerial view shows the Fort Dix Army Air Forces Base. Most of the structures were of the temporary, wooden, mass-produced variety. Today, only a few of these structures remain. The only dormitories of the era belonged to the 108th Air Refueling Wing on the northern part of the base. (McGuire Air Force Base History Office.)

Pegasus

2nd M. A. T. GROUP — FERRYING DIVISION A. T. C.

VOL. 1—NO. 2 | 592 AAFBU | ARMY AIR BASE, FORT DIX, N. J. | Saturday, July 14, 1945

Many F. D. Men to Go Over

Capt. Gallivan Appointed New 1-E Head

Capt. J. P. Gallivan, formerly Special Service head at Memphis Army Air Base, has arrived at this base to take over Information and Education. A veteran of both world wars, Capt. Gallivan returned recently from the China Burma India theatre where he had a roving assignment to establish Information Centers and lecture on War Information.

As a member of the 26th Division in World War 1 (the famous Yankee Division) and as a captain in Administration with the Air Transport Command, he has won six battle stars.

Originally with the 10th Air Force, Capt. Gallivan was requested by ATC when the CBI Wing was activated for War information work.

Calcutta, Accra, Assam and Bombay were but a few of the bases from which he went to his front line assignments.

In discussing the Japanese soldier as a fighting man, Capt. Gallivan stated, "He is good, but not equal to the yank." He added, "Besides production and utilization of machines another distinct advantage is the intelligent initiative of the American G.I." He further stated, "Orientation contributes in some degree to developing that initiative. Studies made of troops in the ETO show that Orientation was a valuable training aid, as many of the discussions directly concerned combat."

With a larger and more comprehensive schedule in I and E work as a goal, Capt. Gallivan said, "Our job is not combat but logistics and intelligent initiative is of even greater importance in getting that job done."

REDUCED RATIONS

If you're planning on getting fat in the army you'd better change your mind because the Quartermaster issue on meat and fish has been cut between 20 and 30%. But don't be alarmed because you'll still get you're vitamins, or in army parlance, your caloric content.

The QM issue per 100 men for 1945 was from 115 to 130 lbs. of meat or fish per day. This has now been cut to 85 lbs., which brings a big problem to the mess section. Capt. Burton Rose, Mess Officer stated; "Everything possible is being done for you by the mess section and as Quartermaster menus are planned to include all things necessary for a balanced diet, don't worry about not getting enough to eat."

445th Veterans Arrive For Reassignment

The most recent Eighth Air Force unit to arrive at the Air Base for reassignment is the 445th Bombardment Group, commanded by Colonel William C. Jones.

Following closely on the heels of the 453rd Bombardment Group, now in the course of processing, members of the 445th (B-24 Liberators), veterans of more than 18 months overseas, will be assigned to various Air Transport Command installations throughout the country.

"SONG OF MEDICS"

Shown above is a scene from "Song of the Medics," musical extravaganza which played at Fort Dix Army Air Base last week. Produced by the Reconditioning Service-Tilton General Hospital in collaboration with the Special Service Office of Fort Dix. The "Medic" show was well received. Story on page 4.

Noted Red 'China' Author To Speak On Base Soon

Mr. Harrison Forman, noted author of "Report From Red China," who recently returned from an extensive tour throughout the Chinese Communist area, has been invited by the I-E Office to speak at the Base Theatre. He will speak on two occasions; Tuesday, July 17th, at 1600 and on Wednesday, July 18th, at 900. All Officers and EM's may attend either of the lectures.

Harrison Forman author of the recently published book, REPORT FROM RED CHINA, is a noted author, lecturer and explorer. He was in China from 1941 until Christmas 1944, having returned to this country six mbonths ago. During the last five months of his stay in China he visited the Chinese Communists, the first foreign correspondent permitted to enter that area of north China.

When Pearl Harbor was attacked December, 1941, Mr. Forman was in Chunking as correspondent from China for the New York Times, London Times, and National Broadcasting Company.

He spent 15 years in the Far East, first journeying to China in 1931 to sell commercial aircraft to the Chinese government.

As explorer, Mr. Forman, undertook three expeditions to Tibet, in 1932, 1935 and 1937. He was a war correspondent of Sino-Jap hostilities in Shangai in 1932, and later that year organized and led a motor caravan expedition to Central Asia. The same year he was the first white man to drive a motor car to the shores of Lake Kokonor, Tibet.

The only war correspondent to be present at the outbreak of both the European and Pacific Wars, in Shangai and in Warsaw, Mr. Forman took motion pictures of both the Jap bombardment of Shangai—1937, and the German bombardment of Warsaw, Poland 1939. The former were released through March of Time, 1937. He also took motion pictures of the Chinese Communist Red Army—1937, and of Russo-Jap hostilities at Changefung Hill on Siberia-Manchukuo-Korea border—1938.

Mr. Forman worked for Columbia Pictures in Hollywood for one year as technical director of the motion picture, LOST HORIZONS.

Golf Ball Ban Lifted

A sizeable group of our population—the golf players—has a special reason for celebrating. The War Production Board recently announced that the ban laid down on the manufacture of golf balls, in 1942, has been lifted.

Of 224,000 dozen golf balls now being turned out quarterly, 94,000 dozen will be earmarked for military use. One fact, however, to temper the joy of players is that even such new balls as are manufactured probably will not be available until next spring.

Walter Wood, of A. G. Spalding, famous sporting-goods house, advises golfers to be patient. "For three years we have been making no golf balls and now our plant at Chicopee, Mass., must be re-geared to the new order."

The new balls, Mr. Wood reveals, will have a synthetic rubber core. Whether this will detract from or add to their playability is a question which will be answered only upon the fairways of the nation.

Helicopters Used for Rescue Work in China

(ALNS)—Personnel of the army that has been strained in remote and otherwise inaccessible areas in China, is being rescued by the use of helicopters that have been shipped to the Orient for that purpose. Many persons, injured when they have been forced to bail out of planes in mountainous areas, have been rescued and given hospital treatment within a short time by the use of the helicopters.

Returnees Will Replace Field Personnel Here

"Personnel classified as returnees will not be assigned overseas on a permanent change of station until all available qualified non-returnee personnel in the same military occupational specialty have been so assigned, unless returnees voluntarily request reassignment in writing," stated Brig. Gen. Bob E. Noland, commanding general of the Ferrying Division, ATC, in a recent letter addressed to this air base.

The letter further read: "Pilots with primary military occupation specialties other than pilot duties, such as Operations Officer, Inspector, Instructor, Engineering etc., will be considered in the pilot MOS insofar as overseas assignment is concerned. Exceptions to this rule will be made only by this headquarters and on a temporary basis when transfer in other than pilot MOS is imminent."

"Under present headquarters ATC plans," continued General Noland, "it is anticipated that all pilots in the Ferrying Division who have not had a minimum of six months on overseas duty on PCS and who are qualified for overseas assignment in accordance with existing directives, will be assigned by approximately August 15, 1945.

"It is incumbent upon all station commanders to immediately train returnees to replace pilot personnel now filling administrative jobs. In the future, when personnel is requested by name or MOS from a station for an overseas assignment, it is expected that a returnee will have been trained as a replacement."

It was further pointed out that "the rate of assignment overseas in other than pilot MOS's varies. Radio Operator Mechanics (2756) are already being reassigned for a second tour of duty. Assignment of ground officers and enlisted men, with the exception of Radio Operator Mechanics has been sharply reduced in view of the redeployment of overseas forces.

"However, it is anticipated that on or about September 1, 1945, the assignment of this personnel to overseas theatres will rapidly increase. As yet no definite data for completion of the initial overseas assignment of all other pilot MOS's can be given. It is urged, that returnees be trained as replacements in all MOS's as quickly as possible."

General Nowland's letter concluded with the following note. "Length of domestic duty since return from overseas will be the basis for reassignment within each MOS of returnees when a second overseas tour of duty for returnees becomes necessary . . . Personnel with the longest period of duty will be reassigned first.

"Consistant with military necessity, individuals assigned overseas for a second tour of duty will be given an opportunity to state thei[r] preference as to the theatre assi[gn]ment. It should be remem[bered] that the overall requirem[ents of] the war effort must re[main the] final determining facto[r]

The Story of Ferd

This is the second installment in a series of eighteen articles dealing with the Ferrying Division and its various installations.

In the three years, since July, 1942, Fort Dix Air Base has been under six different commands. The 1st Air Force took over the base in July, 1942, retaining jurisdiction until October of that year when the Air Service Command took over. Anti-submarine missions were flown from the base concurrently with other ASC activities in December, 1942. In January, 1943, the base came under the Middletown Air Depot Control Area of ASC.

In August of the same year the Second Electronics Experimental Detachment transferred from Mitchell Field to the Fort Dix Field to conduct cross country and experimental flights. In January, 1944, the base was reassigned to the Atlantic Overseas Air Service Command and its main mission was overhauling, servicing and packaging of planes for overseas shipments.

On May 1, 1944, the tFirs Air Force again assumed the command of the field and its mission was the highly secialized bombardment training for selected personnel of the AAF. On September 8, 1944, another mission was added when training was started for the use of Ground Control Approach radar equipment. GCA enables an aircraft to make a safe approach to a runway under conditions approaching zero visibility.

Arrival of ATC planes is not new to the Fort Dix base, for air evacuation planes have been using the field regularly. Tilton General Hospital is located at Fort Dix. However, it was not until 1 June 1945 that the Ferrying Division ATC assumed complete jurisdiction of the field with Lt. Col. Stanley J. Young as Commanding Officer. Under the 1st Air Force, Fort Dix was commanded by Col. Lloyd T. Jones from November, 1943, until the Ferrying Division assumed jurisdiction.

Fort Dix Army Air Base is to the Atlantic Coast what Stockton AAF is to the Pacific. It is the eastern terminal of the M-A-T line which has as its three big jobs: (1) transportation of stragetic and priority cargoes; (2) air evacuation of wounded and (3) crew transport.

The *Pegasus* served the Fort Dix Army Air Base community during World War II until mid-1946, when no one remained to keep the newspaper going.

BASE
OPERATIONS

BASE
OPERATIONS

AIRCRAFT
CLEARANCE
—HERE—

IELD
EVATION
20 FT.

The base operations building in mid–World War II was a simple utilitarian structure, indicating that McGuire was never envisioned as a key postwar facility. This photograph has been reproduced often in the base's history. (McGuire Air Force Base History Office.)

Fort Dix Army Air Forces Base served as a major staging base for units on their way to Europe during the first three years of the war. Many of these faces from the officers club would serve in Europe during the last year of the war. (Fort Dix Museum Archives.)

The Military Police Detachment is pictured in 1943. (Fort Dix Museum Archives.)

The Signal Detachment personnel of Fort Dix Army Airfield have a modern-day equivalent mission with the 305th Communications Squadron. (Fort Dix Museum Archives.)

The officers club was the hub of activities for fliers and local dignitaries at Fort Dix Army Air Forces Base. Its interior appointments belied the temporary nature of its construction. (McGuire Air Force Base History Office.)

Sfc. Zola Marcus, an accomplished commercial artist, painted many murals around the air base. Shown in mid-1943, this mural depicts U.S. Army Air Forces aircraft of the day. (McGuire Air Force Base History Office.)

Fort Dix Army Air Forces Base served as a key development area for early guided weapons during 1943 and 1944 with the 2nd Army Air Forces Electronic Experimentation Unit and numerous detachments. Here, a B-17F launches an early glide bomb. (McGuire Air Force Base History Office.)

With the end of World War II, Fort Dix Army Air Forces Base served as a demobilization base for the U.S. Army Air Forces. Many units returned to New Jersey on their way to inactive status—a reversal for a base that had been a primary waypoint for forces bound for Europe. Camp Kilmer in New Brunswick, New Jersey, had served almost exclusively in that capacity as well. (McGuire Air Force Base History Office.)

Three

THE LEGACY OF
THOMAS B. MCGUIRE JR.

Airmen in formation are a continuous part of an air force base. Early in McGuire's history, it was not unusual to see several varieties of uniforms. Only after the Korean War did the U.S. Air Force throw off the last vestiges of the U.S. Army Air Forces.

As World War II wound down, civil engineers prepared the base for mothball status and closure by October 1946. The aerial photographs on these two pages are from that time. Because the base was built as a temporary expansion base, no one in the War Department foresaw the need

to keep Fort Dix Army Air Forces Base open. The coming cold war put to rest such demobilization hopes. (McGuire Air Force Base History Office.)

The Fort Dix Army Air Base main gate faced Wrightstown and remained the standard entry until the mid-1950s. (McGuire Air Force Base History Office.)

The cold war caused a reevaluation of the nation's defenses, as it became obvious that the Soviet Union had become a significant threat to postwar complacency. As the U.S. Air Force became a separate and autonomous service, Strategic Air Command made it known that it wanted the former Fort Dix Army Forces Base for long-range reconnaissance and strategic bombers. Newly constructed Hangar 1801 was large enough to accommodate bombers and large transport aircraft and was permanent in design. (McGuire Air Force Base History Office.)

Maj. Thomas B. McGuire Jr., originally from Ridgewood, was the second leading all-time American ace and the highest-scoring American pilot ever lost in combat. McGuire received the Congressional Medal of Honor posthumously in 1946. He was a virtuosic pilot and headed a distinguished group of New Jersey airmen who achieved greatness in World War II. Upon his death on January 7, 1945, the War Department searched for a suitable base to name for him. He had grown to maturity in Sebring, Florida (which also claimed him as its own), after his parents separated in the mid-1930s. (McGuire Air Force Base History Office.)

WESTERN UNION

A. N. WILLIAMS
PRESIDENT

1220

Tommy

The filing time shown in the date line on telegrams and day letters is STANDARD TIME at point of origin. Time of receipt is STANDARD TIME at point of destination

NY102 LG PD=BU WASHINGTON DC 20 815A

1946 FEB 20 AM 8 56

CITY EDITOR

PATERSON EVENING NEWS

FOR IMMEDIATE RELEASE STOP REPRESENTATIVE J. PARNELL
THOMAS, NEW JERSEY, TODAY ANNOUNCED HE HAD BEEN INFORMED
THAT THE MEDAL OF HONOR, THE HIGHEST AWARD CONGRESS CAN
BESTOW FOR HEROISM IN ACTION, WILL BE AWARDED POSTHUMOUSLY
TO THE LATE MAJOR THOMAS E. MCGUIRE, JR., SON OF THOMAS B.
MCGUIRE, SR., RIDGEWOOD AUTOMOBILE DEALER. MAJOR MCGUIRE,
THE NATION'S RANKING ACTIVE AIR ACE AT THE TIME OF HIS DEATH,
WAS SHOT DOWN AND KILLED IN THE PHILIPPINES ON JANUARY 7,
1945. AT THE TIME OF HIS DEATH HE HAD SHOT DOWN 38 JAP
PLANES, A RECORD EXCEEDED ONLY BY THE LATE MAJOR RICHARD I.
BONG, OF POPLAR, WISC., WHO WAS CREDITED WITH 40 PLANES.
MAJOR BONG, WHO HELD THE MEDAL OF HONOR, WAS KILLED IN AN
AIR ACCIDENT IN THIS COUNTRY. REP. THOMAS DECLARED HE WAS
MAKING AN EFFORT TO HAVE THE AWARD PRESENTED TO MEMBERS OF
MAJOR MCGUIRE'S FAMILY IN THE WHITE HOUSE, BY PRESIDENT
TRUMAN. HE SAID NO DATE HAD BEEN SET FOR THE PRESENTATION,
BUT EXPRESSED HOPE THAT IT WOULD BE ANNOUNCED SOON. MAJOR
MCGUIRE'S WIDOW, WHOM HE MARRIED WHILE HE WAS IN TRAINING,
LIVES IN SAN ANTONIO, AND, IN THE EVENT THE PRESENTATION
TAKES PLACE IN THE WHITE HOUSE, BOTH SHE AND THE AIR HERO'S
FATHER WILL BE PRESENT AT THE CEREMONY. MRS. MCGUIRE HAS
ALREADY RECEIVED A LETTER FROM MAJOR GENERAL KENNETH B. WOLF,
COMMANDING THE FIFTH AIR FORCE, CONGRATULATING HER ON THE =

This War Department telegram addresses McGuire's Medal of Honor conferral.

Legendary airman Charles Lindbergh (left) flew with the 475th Fighter Group, and McGuire (right) flew on several missions with him. The two became fast friends, and Lindbergh attended the solemn presentation ceremonies for McGuire's posthumous Medal of Honor. Anne Morrow Lindbergh was a stalwart supporter of the P-38 memorial later dedicated on the base. (McGuire Air Force Base History Office.)

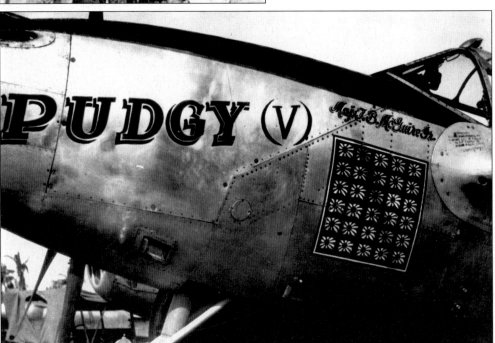

McGuire named his aircraft *Pudgy* in homage to his wife, Marilynn, who was given the unflattering nickname in jest by friends in San Antonio, Texas, when she wore a tight dress as a schoolgirl. McGuire did not feel that the nickname fit his wife, but it certainly proved apropos for the unusual contours of the P-38. He scored his last 13 victories in *Pudgy V*, shown here. (McGuire Air Force Base History Office.)

A little-known fact is that McGuire was not killed in *Pudgy V*, but rather in Capt. Fred Champlin's *Eileen Anne*. This formation shot of the 431st aircraft over the Philippines in late 1944 shows aircraft 112—probably the same aircraft in which McGuire lost his life. (McGuire Air Force Base History Office.)

Thomas B. McGuire Sr., father of the late ace, became a fixture at the base named for his son. The base gave him quarters when he visited, and he had his own office late in life. He became been a tremendous supporter of the U.S. Air Force. As the air force drew up plans for the reopening of the air base at Fort Dix, Congress approved the name McGuire Air Force Base on January 13, 1948. (McGuire Air Force Base History Office.)

MᴄGUIRE AIR FIELD
SOUTHWEST MINDORO, P.I.

The first McGuire Army Air Base was in Mindoro, Republic of the Philippines, in 1945–1946. Mindoro Field was in the area of Thomas McGuire Jr.'s final post in the Philippines and closed shortly after World War II. Scrapped aircraft can be seen in the lower right-hand corner of the field. (McGuire Air Force Base History Office.)

Pudgy V is pictured before the kill board was increased to accommodate up to 42 aerial victories. McGuire (left) is shown with his commander, Col. Charles McDonald, 475th Fighter Group. (McGuire Air Force Base History Office.)

Pudgy IV was a P-38 J in which McGuire scored his 22nd victory. Victories 23 through 38 were achieved in *Pudgy V*. (McGuire Air Force Base History Office.)

Thomas McGuire Sr. owned a Packard dealership in Paterson, New Jersey, pictured in an early-1938 photograph. His only son drove Packard automobiles in Sebring, Florida, and was known as something of a daredevil behind the wheel. His father lavished gifts and attention on him.

In 1982, the newly acquired memorial *Pudgy V* was hoisted in place on its new pedestal. (McGuire Air Force Base History Office.)

McGuire's memorial P-38L-5 (shown here before its transfer to Mcguire and subsequent pedestal status) performed a stunning aerial display during the P-38 40th-anniversary reunion. Pictured, from left to right, are legends Gen. Ben Kelsey, Kelly Johnson, and Tony LeVier. (McGuire Air Force Base History Office.)

Thomas McGuire Sr. (left) and Charles Lindbergh confer during the posthumous Medal of Honor presentation ceremony in 1946. (McGuire Air Force Base History Office.)

The 91st Strategic Reconnaissance Wing began B-29 operations at McGuire in July 1948 during the height of the Berlin Airlift crisis. From that time forward, the base's strategic location or key missions kept the base on the front line of America's air defense (the unit moved to the Pacific for the Korean War in 1950). (McGuire Air Force Base History Office.)

Maj. Thomas B. McGuire Jr. received the Congressional Medal of Honor posthumously in August 1946 in a citation signed by Pres. Harry S. Truman. McGuire's wife, Marilynn (who unfortunately never saw her new husband again after July 1943), Charles Lindbergh (left), Gen. George Kenney (right, commander of Strategic Air Command after the war), and other dignitaries gathered in Ridgewood for the presentation of the medal on May 5, 1946. (McGuire Air Force Base History Office.)

Three duplicate sets of McGuire's medals were produced. The elder McGuire and his son's widow became less than amicable once she remarried; thus, everything done for the family had to be done separately for the most part by the U.S. Air Force. Marilynn donated much of the original memorabilia from her husband's career to the U.S. Air Force Museum in Dayton, Ohio, and her set of medals to the small memorial to her husband at the Sebring Public Library in Florida. Thus are there three shrines to the memory of the legendary major. This is the McGuire Welcome Center c. 1993. (McGuire Air Force Base History Office.)

Four

THE COLD WAR AND MANY MISSIONS

The unsuitability of McGuire to sustain the operations of the heavy B/RB-29s and B-50s, along with a desire to base them in harder-to-reach locations, caused the U.S. Air Force to move bombers away from the base in favor of the more logical air-defense fighters—McGuire's strategic location to thwart air attacks on the major cities of the Northeast taking precedent. On October 1, 1949, McGuire became a facility of the 1st Air Force, Continental Air Command. F-82 Twin Mustangs of the 52nd Fighter Wing (All Weather) began to supplant the heavy bombers by midyear. (McGuire Air Force Base History Office.)

On September 1, 1950, McGuire transferred to the Eastern Air Defense Force. The move was part of an overall effort to streamline and coordinate the nation's air defenses to prevent or disrupt a Soviet attack. McGuire's first jet fighters, the F-94A Starfire (and later the C variant) arrived at this time, equipping no fewer than four squadrons. (McGuire Air Force Base History Office.)

The 52nd Fighter Wing (All Weather) inactivated in February 1952, replaced by the Eastern Air Defense Force–controlled 4709th Air Defense Wing. They flew F-82s and F-94s for much of their McGuire history. (McGuire Air Force Base History Office.)

The 141st Fighter Bomber Squadron (of the 108th Fighter Bomber Wing, Newark Airport), flying F-47 Thunderbolts, was assigned to McGuire in December 1951. A component of the 108th Fighter Wing (now Air Refueling Wing), the Air National Guard has been a fixture at McGuire ever since. (McGuire Air Force Base History Office.)

The New Jersey Air National Guard took possession of many of the temporary barracks on the older parts of the base. Construction of permanent facilities began in 1955. (McGuire Air Force Base History Office.)

A seismic shift began to take hold of McGuire after the conclusion of the active air campaigns of the Korean War in July 1953. McGuire's easy access to the Atlantic flying routes for passenger and cargo aircraft made it an ideal candidate for the Military Air Transport Service. The U.S. Air Force rendered that decision in July 1954, and the 1611th Air Transport Wing was activated. C-54 Skymasters, made famous by the Berlin Airlift, were the first cargo aircraft assigned. The historic 18th Air Transport Squadron, the Blue Diamonds, was the first regular airlift squadron assigned. (McGuire Air Force Base History Office.)

This parade, held on July 27, 1954, commemorated the 1611th Air Transport Wing activation. The most significant cold war changes at McGuire were the activation of the 1611th Air Transport Wing in 1954 and the move of the Atlantic Division, Military Air Transport Service headquarters (later renamed 21st Air Force) to McGuire in April 1955. At the same time, McGuire became the aerial port of embarkation for the eastern United States. Thousands of military personnel passed through McGuire thereafter. The new mission helped solidify the base's position in the U.S. Air Force. (McGuire Air Force Base History Office.)

The first airlift aircraft assigned to McGuire for its new mission was a C-54 like this one. On September 2, 1954, the 18th Air Transport Squadron performed the first-ever airlift mission based out of McGuire—Operation Ice Cube, an airlift of dry ice from Newark to Boston to help in the wake of power outages from a hurricane. Doing the honors was a C-54. (McGuire Air Force Base History Office.)

In late 1954, the first C-118 Liftmaster arrived at McGuire and was assigned to the 18th Air Transport Squadron, flying its first missions in January. The C-118 is a remarkable aircraft and still indeed serves the nation as a fire-suppression aircraft and still handles passengers in its DC-6B guise. (McGuire Air Force Base History Office.)

Soon after arriving at McGuire, the Atlantic Division of the Military Air Transport Service recorded its 25,000th flight. On board the historic flight were Thomas B. McGuire Sr. and New Jersey Gov. Robert Baumle Meyner (on ramp, left). (McGuire Air Force Base History Office.)

The crew of that historic flight poses here. From left to right are the following: (front row) S.Sgt. George Hilton, A3c. Jayne Deuyter, Lt. Col. Augustus Rapisardi, S.Sgt. Ann John, and A2c. Donald A. Walker; (back row) M.Sgt. Dwayne R. Todd, 1st Lt. Richard Brown, Capt. John Didomineco, Capt. Keith Christensen, 1st Lt. Melvin T. Deschamps, and T.Sgt. Donald Holland. (McGuire Air Force Base History Office.)

The C-118 Liftmaster (on static display near the base's passenger terminal) served almost 10 years at McGuire, from March 1955 to April 1964. It was then transferred to the U.S. Navy, which flew the aircraft until June 1, 1982. The navy renumbered the aircraft 152687 and continued to fly it as a long-distance transport until transferring it to the U.S. Air Force Museum. This aircraft was almost certainly the plane that brought Sgt. Elvis Presley back to the United States from Germany when he departed active duty on March 3, 1960. (McGuire Air Force Base History Office.)

GUEST REGISTRATION CARD
VISITING OFFICERS QUARTERS
McGuire Air Force Base, N. J.
PLEASE PRINT

PRESLEY ELVIS- NMI   US-S-926778,

Last Name   First Name   Grade (Mil. or Civ.)   Serial No.

3 rd Army

Organization or Permanent Address — APO or City, State, Country

Home —   269   3MCH

Destination   Flight No.   Flight Date

STATUS

- [x] **PASSENGER**
- [ ] **GUEST**
- [ ] **ACFT CREW**
- [ ] **TDY**
- [ ] **ORD LEAVE**

- [ ] **PCS**
- [x] **SEPARATION**
- [ ] **MORALE LEAVE**
- [ ] **EMERGENCY LEAVE**
- [ ] **OTHER**

Presley Elvis

Guest Signature

McGuire's air passenger terminal, shown in 1956, was considered the U.S. Air Force's "Eastern Gateway to Europe." The terminal processed more than 169,000 passengers in the first half of 1956 alone. (McGuire Air Force Base History Office.)

McGuire Air Force Base, as did all major U.S. bases, received a comprehensive photographic inventory of its facilities. The images document a base brought back to life using many temporary structures from World War II interspersed with new facilities. Shown here is the heavy maintenance hangar in 1954. (McGuire Air Force Base History Office.)

The control tower is pictured prior to modernization in the 1960s.

This 1954 photograph shows the base exchange, which housed the Civilian Cafe.

54

The new base structural fire station is shown in 1954.

This photograph from 1954 shows the distinguished visitor's quarters. Thomas McGuire Sr. stayed here on occasion.

The Civilian Cafe, in the base exchange building, is pictured in 1954.

The alert hangars (the base's primary reason for being in the early 1950s) remained a viable portion of the base through the 1960s.

This 1954 photograph offers an interior view of the Air Defense Command alert hangar.

The airmen's mess is pictured in 1954.

The base dispensary building is shown in 1954.

The New Jersey Air National Guard used the World War II mobility structures as headquarters office space in 1954.

The base library, pictured in 1954, was a creatively adapted building. Now housed in Building 2603 beside the new dining facility, the library was nicely renovated in the 1990s.

The base gymnasium (now a fitness center) is shown in 1954. A major construction project was later implemented to replace much of the facility by 2004.

The officers club, shown in 1954, was housed in Building 3535. A new 28,500-square-foot permanent facility opened in 1971 and remains in use, complementing the new enlisted club, which opened in 1989. The old club, an open-mess system, had included officers, airmen, noncommissioned officers, and senior noncommissioned officers at its peak during the 1960s. Reduction in numbers of personnel, as well as a need for the clubs to pay their own way, led to the streamlined system of today—an enlisted and an officers club.

The headquarters of the Eastern Transport Air Force, located in Building 2901, became the airlift wing headquarters after 1973. (McGuire Air Force Base History Office.)

The first major crisis to which McGuire's aircraft responded was Operation Safe Haven I and II—the evacuation of Hungarian refugees and freedom fighters after the uprising had caused many to seek refuge in nearby Austria, leading to a humanitarian crisis. Pres. Dwight D. Eisenhower offered 15,000 Hungarians asylum in the United States.

Between December 11, 1956, and June 30, 1957, Military Air Transport Service aircraft and some contract aircraft transported more than 14,000 people from Europe to McGuire. On December 21 alone, some 984 refugees were evacuated to McGuire from Munich, Germany. The refugees were transported from McGuire to Camp Kilmer in New Brunswick, New Jersey, to be processed for resettlement in the United States. Safe Haven I and II was the most significant humanitarian operation since the Berlin Airlift. (McGuire Air Force Base History Office.)

The first purpose-built aeromedical airlift aircraft, the C-131 Samaritan, began operations at McGuire in 1955, continuing service with the 12th Aeromedical Transport Squadron until supplanted by the C-141 in 1969. (McGuire Air Force Base History Office.)

Not as well known as the Samaritan in the med-evac role, C-121 Super Constellations were flown by the New Jersey Air National Guard for the mission during the mid-1960s for intertheater airlift during the Vietnam War. (Don Spering.)

The U.S. Navy had a robust part of the airlift mission at McGuire, flying its R4D-8 (C-47) and R6D. McGuire later became one of the first bases equipped with the C-130E Hercules. Squadrons VR-3 and VR-6 flew from McGuire until the phaseout of the C-130E in 1968. (McGuire Air Force Base History Office.)

The robust F-86D Sabre Dog had an extensive history at McGuire, flying from 1953 to 1959, when it was replaced by the F-102A. Aircraft of the 2nd and 5th Fighter Interceptor Squadrons were photographed often. (Don Spering.)

The F-102A Delta Dagger flew from McGuire in defense of the Northeast corridor from 1957 to 1959 with the 339th Fighter Interceptor Squadron until it was supplanted by the F-106 Delta Dart. (McGuire Air Force Base History Office.)

Eminent airman Robinson Risner (left), who retired as a brigadier general in 1976, was an ace from the Korean War (eight victories) and was 34th Fighter Squadron commander at George Air Force Base, California, when the U.S. Air Force selected him to commemorate the 40th anniversary of Lindbergh's solo crossing of the Atlantic Ocean in May 1957. He completed the flight in 6 hours and 18 minutes. Pictured at McGuire before the commemorative flight, Risner views weather data with Kenneth Boedecker, Lindbergh's personal mechanic on the historic first flight. (McGuire Air Force Base History Office.)

McGuire produced several historical women, including Grace Peterson, the first woman to become a chief master sergeant in the U.S. Air Force. Peterson (far left) is shown with Col. Rufus Ward (base commander), Capt. Margaret McCaffrey (third from left), and 2d Lt. Mary H. Weldman on September 24, 1957. (McGuire Air Force Base History Office.)

The McGuire chapel stood alone after its completion in 1956. This portion of the base is now one of the most developed, including the officers club, enlisted club, and the 21st Air Force headquarters within a stone's throw of the chapel. (McGuire Air Force Base History Office.)

Because of its proximity to Philadelphia and New York City, McGuire attracted numerous star performers (the New York Knicks used the base for preseason conditioning). At the February 1955 McGuire Air Force Base Mardi Gras, actress Cleo Moore was selected as the queen, and Duke Ellington and his orchestra performed for the festivities. In this view, Ellington clowns on the organ with child virtuoso Glenn Derringer of Philadelphia while Moore dominates the scene. (McGuire Air Force Base History Office.)

Five

JET AIRLIFT
AND THE VIETNAM ERA

In this 1961 view of McGuire, note the large quantity of transport and fighter aircraft to the right. It was a busy time for the base. (McGuire Air Force Base History Office.)

In the mid-1950s, because of McGuire's strategic location, the U.S. Air Force advanced plans to site the nuclear-tipped BOMARC missile at an annex at McGuire. The BOMARC was essentially a computer-directed unmanned fighter plane capable of achieving Mach 3. It would explode near an enemy bomber formation, using either conventional or nuclear warheads. Originally termed F-99, it was redesignated as CIM-99 and then CIM-10. McGuire became the first base ever to field an operational nuclear missile squadron in 1959, when BOMARCs became operational with the 46th Air Defense Missile Squadron. (McGuire Air Force Base History Office.)

The BOMARC annex at McGuire was about 11 miles southeast of the base on Fort Dix Range property. (McGuire Air Force Base History Office.)

Thirty years before it flew humanitarian missions in Operation Enduring Freedom, McGuire helped the people of Afghanistan with an unusual mission to help build dairy cattle stocks in the ravaged region. The November 17, 1962 mission featured McGuire's aerial port technicians loading Brown Swiss cattle onto a C-97 for the transoceanic trek. (McGuire Air Force Base History Office.)

The guest speaker for the 1966 ball at McGuire (the 19th anniversary of the U.S. Air Force) was Gen. Ira Eaker. He had completed his stint as chairman of Douglas Aircraft and had begun a period of lecturing and editorial writing on strategic affairs. (McGuire Air Force Base History Office.)

The Thunderbirds have been regular performers at McGuire Friends and Neighbors Days (open houses). Pictured here with the early-1960s F-100 team, Thomas McGuire Sr. remained a central figure. (McGuire Air Force Base History Office.)

Fairchild C-119 Flying Boxcars are shown at Newark City Airport in January 1957. New Jersey bases were key to the national defense logistical efforts, especially when one factored in Fort Monmouth and the military port at Bayonne.

The C-135A, the transport version of the KC-135, was the U.S. Air Force's first operational all-jet transport aircraft. McGuire scored another first as these aircraft began operations in June 1961, gradually assuming the role of the C-118. Most of the McGuire C-135s were converted to other uses as exotic RC-135s. (McGuire Air Force Base History Office.)

Another first for McGuire was the initial operational capability of its F-106A Delta Daggers of the 539th Fighter Interceptor Squadron. On May 30, 1959, McGuire's own Maj. William H. Champion became the first F-106A pilot to fire an operational Genie missile. (McGuire Air Force Base History Office.)

The Semi-Autonomous Ground Environment (SAGE) computer was the world's first operation digital system with a magnetic memory core. The huge system controlled F-106A and BOMARC missiles at McGuire, and there was a huge theater-status map housed within this giant block building. The 462nd Air Defense Wing, New York Air Defense Sector, controlled the airspace. The 21st Air Force moved into the building in 1973. (McGuire Air Force Base History Office.)

Two of the most important resident fighters of McGuire were the F-84F, which as part of the 108th Tactical Fighter Wing, had a nuclear-delivery capability (phased out in 1964), and the F-105B Thunderchief, which supplanted it within the wing and remained operational until 1982. (McGuire Air Force Base History Office.)

The Air Refueling Wing F-84Fs took part in Operation Stair Step in October 1961, redeploying in expectation of war during the Cuban Missile Crisis. (McGuire Air Force Base History Office.)

On March 16, 1961, the 514th Troop Carrier Wing, Air Force Reserve, and its Fairchild C-119 Flying Boxcars arrived. McGuire is still a super-base in this respect, operating three major wings (active duty, reserve, and Air National Guard) and a numbered air force contingent. (McGuire Air Force Base History Office.)

The first tanker aircraft stationed permanently at McGuire were Boeing KC-97s of the 305th Air Refueling Squadron, dispersed to McGuire from 1960 to 1965. Derived from the Stratofreighter, it shared a name with the later KC-135. (McGuire Air Force Base History Office.)

Times have changed. Thomas McGuire Sr. (sixth from left) and local Paterson business leaders are shown in a mid-1960s cigarette drive. The elder McGuire owned a Packard automobile dealership in Paterson for many years. (McGuire Air Force Base History Office.)

John Levitow, then the lowest-ranking airman (airman first class) to earn the Congressional Medal of Honor in 1969, was stationed at McGuire prior to his posting with the AC-47s in Southeast Asia. A U.S. Air Force statesman and an example to modern-day airmen, he graciously returned to McGuire many times until his death on November 8, 2000. (McGuire Air Force Base History Office.)

The 438th Military Airlift Wing supplanted the 1611th Air Transport Wing in 1966, continuing operations until 1993, when it was replaced by the 305th Air Mobility Wing. (McGuire Air Force Base History Office.)

The C-141 Starlifter became the most important aircraft in McGuire's history. C-141s from nearby Dover started alert duty at McGuire in 1966. (McGuire Air Force Base History Office.)

McGuire's first C-141 (tail No. 66-7947) was christened the *Garden State Starlifter* and arrived on August 7, 1967. (McGuire Air Force Base History Office.)

The C-141 was stretched and converted into an air-refuelable aircraft in the early 1980s. The first C-141B (tail No. 66-0186) served many years at McGuire and stands in the foreground. It was the personal aircraft of the commander in chief of U.S. Transportation Command at Scott Air Force Base, Illinois, and was very much an experimental model; the craft had doors and windows in different locations than all the others. It was rumored that the loading roller mechanism had been installed backwards in the plug extension. (McGuire Air Force Base History Office.)

The C-141B is shown over nearby Manhattan. (McGuire Air Force Base History Office.)

McGuire's commissary and base exchange is shown prior to replacement with the new facility in 1982. (McGuire Air Force Base History Office.)

This photograph, taken in March 1982, shows McGuire's Falcon Courts North family housing. (McGuire Air Force Base History Office.)

On its circuit to Thule, Greenland, McGuire has long dressed its C-141s in holiday garb for Operation Santa Claus (a way to spread goodwill, presents, and mail to remote regions). Shown here is the reindeer-clad No. 67-0007. It was a long-serving McGuire Starlifter and was obviously adorned for the sake of taking this picture. Such accouterment and jet engines do not mix. This photograph is from 1983. (McGuire Air Force Base History Office.)

THE WHITE HOUSE

WASHINGTON

May 12, 1983

Dear Captain Sangiorgio:

I recently learned of your history-making
flight as the commander of the first all-
female U.S. Air Force crew to make a transatlantic crossing. I want to congratulate
not only you but also your entire crew,
including Captain Barbara Akin, First
Lieutenant Terri Ollinger, Staff Sergeant
Donna Wertz, Technical Sergeant Denise
Meunier, Sergeant Mary Eiche and Airman
First Class Bernadette Botti.

Of course, I realize that each member of your
crew has made similar flights before, so flying
across the Atlantic was nothing new for you.
But for the thousands of young women who will
read about your achievement, this flight will
be an inspiration. For that reason, I want to
commend you for what you have done and to
express my confidence that each of you will
go on to many more accomplishments during your
careers in the Air Force.

Please accept my best wishes for every success
and happiness in the future.

Sincerely,

Ronald Reagan

Captain Guiliana Sangiorgio
c/o 18th M.A.S.
McGuire Air Force Base,
  New Jersey 08641

The first all-woman crew to complete a
transatlantic mission (in 1983) received
special praise from Pres. Ronald Reagan.

The crew members were also interviewed on ABC's *Good Morning America.*

Members of the crew are shown at their work stations. Above, S.Sgt. Denise Meunier monitors the flight engineer panel. To the right, Capt. Barbara Akin is at the controls as copilot. (McGuire Air Force Base History Office.)

Col. Larry D. Wright, 438th Military Airlift Wing commander, was instrumental in getting the P-38 to McGuire for the memorial to Major McGuire on Pudgy Circle. He is shown in December 1982 surveying the new C-141B cockpit procedures trainer during its dedication ceremony.

The 21st Air Force took over the SAGE building in 1973 as the BOMARC missile system stood down. (This photograph dates from 1995, when McGuire's buildings had assumed the U.S. Air Force overall beige-brown standard.) Most BOMARCs had already been retired; those that remained finished their career as target drones—thankfully never having been launched in anger. (McGuire Air Force Base History Office.)

Operation Nickel Grass, the airlift of supplies and reinforcements to Israel during the Yom Kippur War between October and November 1973, was a resounding success due in no small part to McGuire's airlift and aerial port facilities. (McGuire Air Force Base History Office.)

The 108th Fighter Wing and the New Jersey Air National Guard had switched to F-4 Phantoms once the venerable F-105Bs had been retired. The "Princeton tiger" logo of the 141st Tactical Fighter Squadron graced their aircraft for a time and remains on the F-4 on static display at McGuire. (Don Spering.)

McGuire's facilities, people, and airlifts again proved essential to Operation New Life after the fall of Saigon in 1975. (McGuire Air Force Base History Office.)

McGuire had attempted to locate and retrieve a P-38 Lightning since at least the mid-1950s. Finally, famous warbird pilot and entrepreneur David Tallichet agreed to trade his flyable P-38L and a P-47 to the U.S. Air Force Museum for display at McGuire for two surplus C-130s. After a taxi accident in Memphis damaged props, McGuire's P-38 arrived on May 25, 1981. With strong community support, the aircraft became a central display feature on base at the newly named Pudgy Circle. (McGuire Air Force Base History Office.)

Every Memorial Day, Pudgy Circle hosts the stirring Parade of Wreaths, in which fallen military and law enforcement officers are honored with wreaths and dedications. (McGuire Air Force Base History Office.)

McGuire's C-141s and the 438th and 514th Military Airlift Wings continued to fly the C-141Bs in support of numerous contingencies and humanitarian operations throughout the world, including Operation Urgent Fury—the Grenada rescue mission. (McGuire Air Force Base History Office.)

The Military Airlift Command hosted biennial "Rodeo" competitions (which still continue under Air Mobility Command). Here, the 438th and 514th Military Airlift Wings' successful 1987 teams hold aloft their trophy for an all-time record score in the "Engine Running On-Load and Off-Load" competition in May 1987. (McGuire Air Force Base History Office.)

McGuire C-141Bs began to receive the Euro I camouflage of green, dark green, and gray (Lizard) in the 1980s. (Don Spering.)

Desert Shield and Desert Storm saw the 438th and 514th Military Airlift Wings C-141B fleet fly more than 102,000 total hours in 3,378 sorties (1990–1991). The end of the cold war meant even harder use for the Starlifters. Here, McGuire's aerial port personnel and C-141s bring vital supplies to the growing Balkan conflict in 1991 at Tirana, Albania. The successful operations portended the end of the C-141B; much of its usable life span used up, it suffered from structural fatigue, and it was obvious that a next-generation airlifter was needed sooner rather than later. For McGuire, with its six squadrons of C-141s, the future looked bleak. Indeed, the Congressional Committee on Base Realignment and Closure recommended McGuire for outright closure by 1995. (McGuire Air Force Base History Office.)

Posing at McGuire in March 1991 are, from left to right, Lee Greenwood, Barbara Eden, Bob Hope, and Connie Stevens. The group entertained at the base during the Gulf War. (McGuire Air Force Base History Office.)

Saving McGuire from closure did spell the end of the 438th Military Airlift Wing. The famous 305th Air Refueling Wing, "Can Do," relocated from Grissom Air Force Base, Indiana, on October 1, 1994, and assumed the role as the host wing and the 305th Air Mobility Wing. Shown here is the activation-inactivation ceremony. (McGuire Air Force Base History Office.)

The reprieve from closure brought about the most significant construction in McGuire's history. The base's aging and antiquated infrastructure received a huge boost, and by decade's end, McGuire was among the best facilities in the U.S. Air Force if not the world. New construction for KC-10s and the air-mobility concept included an expansive control tower and KC-10 campus, along with dormitories, and sundry general-use facilities. (McGuire Air Force Base History Office.)

C-141Bs received their last operational paint scheme of overall neutral gray throughout the 1990s—a concession that the remaining enemies after the cold war were more likely to be ground based. McGuire and some of its select C-141Bs received special operations modifications, including forward-looking infrared radar for the Special Operations Low Level II mission carried out by the Bully Beef 6th Airlift Squadron until October 2002. (McGuire Air Force Base History Office.)

The Air National Guard 170th Refueling Group merged with the 108th Fighter Wing at McGuire in 1992, becoming the 108th Air Refueling Wing. The newly organized wing had two flying squadrons, the 141st and 150th Air Refueling Squadrons, flying the KC-135E. In this late-1990s view, Air National Guard F-16s from Atlantic City provide a striking flyby for the cameras. (McGuire Air Force Base History Office.)

The U.S. Air Force chose to keep the airlift mission at McGuire beyond the projected 2004–2005 retirement of the C-141. In 2001, the air force announced that McGuire was the preferred base for the C-17 Globemaster III. Congress approved money for new C-17 facilities in 2002, and McGuire began yet another transformation to support the hi-tech airlifter. (McGuire Air Force Base History Office.)

106

Part of McGuire's aging infrastructure was its electromagnetic phone switching—here mockingly destroyed for the base newspaper *Airtides*. The all-digital Base Information Digital Distribution system replaced it, readying the base for its new missions and the desktop computer revolution. The system had more computing power than the room-sized Burroughs and IBM systems controlling SAGE in the late 1950s. (McGuire Air Force Base History Office.)

Pres. Jimmy Carter visited McGuire in 1977 shortly after assuming office. (McGuire Air Force Base History Office.)

McGuire's strategic importance was never more important than on September 11, 2001. The base became a critical stop on the nation's road to recovery. In this view, Pres. George W. Bush meets with 305th Air Mobility Wing commander Richard A. Mentemeyer (left) and 21st Air Force commander Maj. Gen. Nick Williams (center) in the tense days immediately following the attack. (McGuire Air Force Base History Office.)

McGuire's personnel and aircraft flew in direct support of almost every part of the war on terrorism. Shown here is a KC-10A, No. 85-0028, upon return from a mission. (McGuire Air Force Base Visual Information.)

McGuire's tanker and airlift aircraft were in action on September 11, 2001. Some tanker aircraft transitioned from training missions to emergency operational-support missions in midair. There was no modern precedent for such operations, but McGuire's personnel performed flawlessly on that sad day. (McGuire Air Force Base Visual Information.)

Brig. Gen. Teresa Marné Peterson assumed command of McGuire on March 1, 2002—the first woman to command the base and the proud 305th Air Mobility Wing. McGuire's history is intertwined with remarkable firsts for women, and General Peterson's selection to become the first woman to command McGuire was a natural progression. (McGuire Air Force Base Visual Information.)

Sen. Bill Bradley from New Jersey once served at McGuire as a reserve comptroller officer within the 514th Air Mobility Wing. He is shown here during a 1984 visit. (McGuire Air Force Base History Office.)

The first documented open house at McGuire was just after V-E Day in 1945. For the first time, the surrounding communities got to tour the base and view their investment in national defense. Open houses continue to this day. This one was in 1957. (McGuire Air Force Base History Office.)

Pictured is an open house in 1963. C-133 Cargomasters, C-124 Globemasters, and an array of fighter aircraft held sway. (McGuire Air Force Base History Office.)

A 1987 open house is shown in this view. In the background, the new F/A-18 Hornets of the Blue Angels await their performance. In the foreground, a C-5B Galaxy from nearby Dover Air Force Base, Delaware, is on static display. The Galaxy was always a crowd pleaser. (McGuire Air Force Base History Office.)

A C-121 Super Constellation, *Lady Diane*, is shown at McGuire in 1973. The Super Constellation served the New Jersey Air National Guard well. It was a fine troop transport, augmenting jet aircraft from the 1950s to the 1970s. It was also arguably one of the finest looking aircraft of its day. (Don Spering.)

Beauty pageants were a fixture of life at most U.S. Air Force bases throughout the 1950s, and McGuire, with Atlantic City and its famous pageant so near, hosted some of the most elaborate ceremonies. Active-duty airmen in the Women's Air Force squadron later competed in Ms. McGuire pageants sponsored by the various squadrons. (McGuire Air Force Base History Office.)

Gen. George Kenney (left) is shown with Thomas McGuire Sr. at the interment of Thomas McGuire Jr. at Arlington National Cemetery in May 1950. General Kenney was one of the staunchest supporters of the younger McGuire and took the death of the second-leading ace especially hard. He pushed for McGuire's posthumous Congressional Medal of Honor. (McGuire Air Force Base History Office.)

AIRCRAFT ASSIGNED TO MCGUIRE AND FORT DIX

DOUGLAS O-46, DECEMBER 30, 1941–JANUARY 3, 1942

104th Observation Squadron	December 30, 1941–January 3, 1942

NORTH AMERICAN O-47, JUNE 9, 1941–OCTOBER 1, 1943

126th Observation Squadron	June 9, 1941–August 27, 1941
59th Observation Group	December 1, 1941–October 18, 1942
104th Observation Squadron	December 30, 1941–January 3, 1942
9th Observation Squadron	April 26, 1942–October 18, 1942
377th Bombardment Group	October 18, 1942–December 9, 1942
516th Bombardment Squadron	October 18, 1942–November 29, 1942
11th Antisubmarine Squadron	November 29, 1942–October 1, 1943

STINSON O-49, JUNE 9, 1941–JANUARY 3, 1942

104th Observation Squadron	December 30, 1941–January 3, 1942
126th Observation Squadron	June 9, 1941–August 27, 1941

CURTIS O-52, MARCH 27, 1942–OCTOBER 1, 1943

119th Observation Squadron	March 27, 1942–August 26, 1942
9th Observation Squadron	April 26, 1942–October 18, 1942
516th Bombardment Squadron	October 18, 1942–November 29, 1942
11th Antisubmarine Squadron	November 29, 1942–October 1, 1943

PIPER O-59, JUNE 9, 1941–AUGUST 26, 1942

104th Observation Squadron	December 30, 1941–January 3, 1942
126th Observation Squadron	June 9, 1941–August 27, 1941
119th Observation Squadron	March 27, 1942–August 26, 1942

CONSOLIDATED B-24 LIBERATOR, MAY 21, 1943–SEPTEMBER 1945

3rd Antisubmarine Squadron	May 21, 1943–September 22, 1943
11th Antisubmarine Squadron	c. August 1943–September 28, 1943
445th Bombardment Group	June 1945–c. September 1945
700th Bombardment Squadron	June 9, 1945–c. September 1945
701st Bombardment Squadron	June 9, 1945–c. September 1945
702nd Bombardment Squadron	June 9, 1945–c. September 1945
703rd Bombardment Squadron	June 9, 1945–c. September 1945
453rd Bombardment Group	June 18, 1945–c. September 1945
732nd Bombardment Squadron	June 18, 1945–c. September 1945
733rd Bombardment Squadron	June 18, 1945–c. September 1945
734th Bombardment Squadron	June 18, 1945–c. September 1945
735th Bombardment Squadron	June 18, 1945–c. September 1945

Note: When the installation was renamed McGuire Air Force Base on January 13, 1948, no U.S. Air Force unit existed on the base. No aircraft were assigned to the installation. No air force unit arrived at McGuire until July 20, 1948. The dedication ceremony on September 17, 1949, is considered by many as the ceremonial or formal dedication of the base.

NORTH AMERICAN B-25 MITCHELL, FEBRUARY 28, 1943–C. AUGUST 1943

3rd Antisubmarine Squadron	February 28, 1943–c. May 1943
11th Antisubmarine Squadron	March 3, 1943–c. August 1943

LOCKHEED B-34 VENTURA, JANUARY 1943–C. MARCH 1943

11th Antisubmarine Squadron	January 1943–c. March 1943

BOEING B/RB-29A SUPERFORTRESS, JULY 20, 1948–SEPTEMBER 21, 1949

91st Strategic Reconnaissance Group	July 20, 1948–October 11, 1948
91st Strategic Reconnaissance Wing	October 11, 1948–October 1, 1949
323rd Reconnaissance Squadron	July 20, 1948–November 10, 1948
324th Reconnaissance Squadron	July 20, 1948–September 21, 1949
16th Photo Reconnaissance Squadron	November 10, 1948–June 1, 1949
323rd Strategic Reconnaissance Squadron	June 1, 1949–September 21, 1949

BOEING B/RB-17 FLYING FORTRESS, AUGUST 17, 1948–C. SEPTEMBER 1949

16th Photo Reconnaissance Squadron	August 1948–November 10, 1948
?	January 22, 1949–June 1, 1949
91st Strategic Reconnaissance Squadron	January 22, 1949–September 21, 1949
91st Strategic Recon Wing (Base Flight)	?–c. September 1949

BOEING B-50A SUPERFORTRESS, JULY 16, 1949–SEPTEMBER 21, 1949

91st Strategic Reconnaissance Squadron	July 16, 1949–September 21, 1949

DOUGLAS C/RC-54G SKYMASTER, ?–C. SEPTEMBER 1949

91st Strategic Recon Wing (Base Flight)	September 1949
18th Air Transport Squadron	August 12, 1954–c. September 1949

NORTH AMERICAN F-82 TWIN MUSTANG, OCTOBER 4, 1949–C. MAY 1950

52nd Fighter Wing	October 4, 1949–January 20, 1950
2nd Fighter Squadron	October 4, 1949–January 20, 1950
5th Fighter Squadron	October 4, 1949–January 20, 1950
84th Fighter Wing (Reserves)	October 10, 1949–January 20, 1950
496th Fighter Squadron (Reserves)	October 10, 1949–January 20, 1950

LOCKHEED F-94A/C STARFIRE, C. MAY 1950–C. MARCH 1953

52nd Fighter-All Weather Wing	c. May 1950–May 1, 1951
2nd Fighter-All Weather Squadron	c. May 1950–May 1, 1951
5th Fighter-All Weather Squadron	c. May 1950–May 1, 1951
84th Fighter-All Weather Wing	c. May 1950–June 1, 1951
496th Fighter-All Weather Squadron	c. May 1950–June 1, 1951
52nd Fighter Interceptor Wing	May 1, 1951–February 6, 1952
4709th Defense Wing	February 6, 1952–January 21, 1953
568th Air Defense Group	January 21, 1953–c. March 1953
2nd Fighter Interceptor Squadron	May 1, 1951–c. February 1953
5th Fighter Interceptor Squadron	May 1, 1951–c. March 1953

REPUBLIC F-47 THUNDERBOLT, DECEMBER 1, 1952–C. JULY 1955
108th Fighter-Bomber Wing (ANG)   December 1, 1952–c. July 1955
141st Fighter-Bomber Squadron   December 1, 1952–c. July 1955

REPUBLIC F-84E/G THUNDERJET, C. FEBRUARY 1953–JULY 18, 1953
2nd Fighter Interceptor Squadron   c. February 1953–July 18, 1953

NORTH AMERICAN F-86A/D/H/L SABRE/SABRE DOG, MARCH 1953–MAY 1959
5th Fighter Interceptor Squadron   c. March 1953–August 18, 1955
2nd Fighter Interceptor Squadron   July 18, 1953–August 18, 1955
141st Fighter Interceptor Squadron   c. July 1955–July 1, 1958
332nd Fighter Interceptor Squadron   August 18, 1955–November 8, 1956
L-539th Fighter Interceptor Squadron   August 18, 1955–c. May 1959
L-332nd Fighter Interceptor Squadron   November 8, 1956–July 1, 1957

DOUGLAS C-54 SKYMASTER, AUGUST 1, 1954–DECEMBER 31, 1964
1611th Air Transport Wing   August 1, 1954–December 31, 1964
18th Air Transport Squadron   August 1, 1954–c. September 1954

DOUGLAS C-118 LIFTMASTER, SEPTEMBER 10, 1954–C. AUGUST 1965
18th Air Transport Squadron   September 10, 1954–June 9, 1961
38th Air Transport Squadron   January 27, 1955–June 25, 1965
Naval Air Transport Squadron 3*   July 16, 1957–January 1964
Naval Air Transport Squadron 6*   April 5, 1955–March 1, 1963
29th Air Transport Squadron   April 13, 1955–c. August 1965
30th Air Transport Squadron   May 16, 1955–June 25, 1965
58th Air Transport Squadron   July 4, 1955–June 18, 1960

CONVAIR C-131 SAMARITAN, APRIL 18, 1955–JUNE 8, 1969
1732nd Air Evacuation Squadron   April 18, 1955–November 8, 1956
12th Aeromedical Transport Squadron   November 8, 1956–June 8, 1969

DOUGLAS R4D-8 SKYTRAIN (C-47), JUNE 13, 1955–C. 1957
Naval Transport Squadron 6   June 13, 1955–c. 1957

BEECH JRB-4 EXPEDITER (C-45), JUNE 13, 1955–C. 1957
Naval Transport Squadron 6   June 13, 1955–c. 1957

DOUGLAS C-47 SKYTRAIN, C. JULY 1955–C. 1957
1611th Field Maintenance Squadron   c. July 1955–c. 1957

BEECH C-45 EXPEDITER, C. JULY 1955
1611th Field Maintenance Squadron   c. July 1955–c. 1957

CONVAIR F-102A DELTA DAGGER, JULY 1, 1957–JULY 9, 1959
332nd Fighter Interceptor Squadron   July 1, 1957–July 9, 1959

LOCKHEED T-33A SHOOTING STAR, JUNE 1958–JANUARY 1963
1611th Operations Squadron   June 1958–January 1963

*The U.S. Navy VR-6 flew the Douglas R6D, an equivalent of the U.S. Air Force Douglas C-118.

Republic F-84F Thunderstreak, July 1, 1958–April 1, 1964
141st Tactical Fighter Squadron   July 1, 1958–April 1, 1964

Cessna U-3A, January 1959–June 1959
1611th Operations Squadron   January 1959–June 1959

Convair F-106A Delta Dart, May 5, 1959–August 31, 1967
539th Fighter Interceptor Squadron   May 5, 1959–August 31, 1967

Convair T-29A Flying Classroom, January 1960–June 1962
1611th Operations Squadron   January 1960–June 1962

Boeing KC-97L Stratotanker, January 15, 1960–March 25, 1965
305th Air Refueling Squadron   January 15, 1960–March 25, 1965

Fairchild C-119 Flying Boxcar, March 15, 1961–September 1970
514th Troop Carrier Wing   March 15, 1961–September 1970
335th Military Airlift Squadron   March 15, 1961–July 1, 1970

Boeing C-135A Stratolifter, June 9, 1961–November 20, 1967
18th Air Transport Squadron   June 9, 1961–June 15, 1966
40th Air Transport Squadron   January 8, 1962–November 20, 1967

Lockheed C-130E Hercules, January 8, 1964–August 31, 1968
Air Transport Squadron 3 (VR-3)   January 1964–July 1, 1968
29th Air Transport Squadron   May 1, 1964–August 31, 1968
45th Military Airlift Squadron   July 1, 1967–August 31, 1968

Republic F-105B Thunderchief, April 1, 1964–1982
141st Tactical Fighter Squadron   April 1, 1964–1982

Lockheed C-121C/G Super Constellation, July 1, 1965–July 15, 1966
150th Air Transport Squadron   July 1, 1965–July 15, 1966

Lockheed C-141A/B Starlifter, August 7, 1967–present
6th Airlift Squadron   April 8, 1970–present
13th Airlift Squadron   October 1, 1993–April 1, 2001
18th Airlift Squadron   August 1, 1968–July 1, 1995
30th Airlift Squadron   August 8, 1967–October 1, 1993
335th Airlift Squadron   April 1, 1970–September 30, 1995
702nd Airlift Squadron   April 1, 1970–April 1, 2001
732nd Airlift Squadron   April 1, 1970–present

Douglas KC-10 Extender, September 1, 1994–present
2nd Air Refueling Squadron   September 1, 1994–present
32nd Air Refueling Squadron   September 1, 1994–present
76th Air Refueling Squadron   September 1, 1994–present
78th Air Refueling Squadron   September 1, 1994–present

Beechcraft C-12F Huron, October 4, 1994–September 26, 1995
32nd Air Refueling Squadron   October 4, 1994–September 26, 1995